CITY CYCLING
PARIS

Rapha.

♻ **Thames & Hudson**

Created by Andrew Edwards and Max Leonard of
Tandem London, a design, print and editorial studio

Thanks to Louis Thomas for illustrations;
Kim Laidlaw and Hugo Mendez; and Greg and
Alexandre Vermersch for racing and training info

First published in the United Kingdom in 2013 by
Thames & Hudson Ltd, 181A High Holborn, London WC1V 7QX

City Cycling Paris © 2013 Andrew Edwards and Max Leonard
Illustrations © 2013 Thames & Hudson Ltd, London and Rapha Racing Ltd

Designed by Andrew Edwards

Illustrations by Louis Thomas, louist.blogspot.co.uk

British Library Cataloguing-in-Publication Data
A catalogue record for this book is available from the British Library

ISBN 978-0-500-29101-6

Printed and bound in China by Everbest Printing Co Ltd

To find out about all our publications, please visit
www.thamesandhudson.com. There you can subscribe
to our e-newsletter, browse or download our current catalogue,
and buy any titles that are in print.

CONTENTS

HOW TO USE THIS GUIDE

This Paris volume of the *City Cycling* series is designed to give you the confidence to explore the city by bike at your own pace. On the front flaps is a locator map of the whole city to help you orient yourself. Here, you will see five neighbourhoods to explore: Louvre, Les Halles (p. 10); Martyrs, Pigalle, Montmartre (p. 16); Canal St-Martin (p. 22); Haut Marais (p. 28); and the Rive Gauche (p. 34). All are easily accessible by bike, and are full of cafés, bars, galleries, museums, shops and parks. Each area is mapped in detail, and our recommendations for places of interest and where to fuel up on coffee and cake, as well as where to find a Wi-Fi connection, are marked. Take a pootle round on your bike and see what suits you.

For maps of the whole city, turn to the back. These detailed maps show bike routes, and roads to avoid, across a large section of central Paris. They'll help you navigate safely, and pinpoint everything you need, from bike shops to Vélib docking stations, landmarks and more. If you fancy a set itinerary, turn to A Day On The Bike on the front flaps. It takes you on a relaxed 35km (22-mile) route through some of the parts of Paris we haven't featured in the neighbourhood sections, and visits some of the more touristy sights. Pick and choose the bits you fancy, go from back to front, and use the route as it suits you.

A section on Racing and Training (p. 40) fills you in on the Tour de France's visits to Paris and more, and provides ideas for longer rides if you want to explore the beautiful countryside around the city, while Essential Bike Info (p. 44) discusses road etiquette and the ins and outs of using the cycle-hire scheme and public transportation. Finally, Links and Addresses (p. 48) will give you the practical details you need to know.

PARIS: THE CYCLING CITY

Combine romantic sophistication, effortless chic and a glorious cycling history unparalleled in any other city, and you have perhaps the ultimate city cycling destination. Whether you're interested in watching the Tour de France arrive on the Champs-Elysées, taking lazy rides along the river or hopping from boulangerie to art gallery, *parfumier* to museum, antiques shop to bistro, it's all possible in the French capital. But there's no question that, in years past, cycling in Paris has appeared intimidating, with the local drivers' aggressive reputation probably keeping many visitors off the roads. As much as it's fun pretending to be Mark Cavendish, and sprinting around the place de la Concorde for the finish, there are a few unpleasant roads in Paris – and the Arc de Triomphe isn't something you'll want to be riding around unless you're an experienced cyclist. Check our maps for details of roads on which we particularly recommend exercising caution, and Essential Bike Info for more safety and security tips.

Warning out of the way, it's time to accentuate the positives. Parisians' attitudes towards cycling have been changing, and the capital now has an extensive and fairly rational system of cycle lanes, many of which are completely separate from the road traffic. This situation will continue to improve – in no small part thanks to the enlightened actions of Paris's mayor, Bertrand Delanoë. In charge of the city since 2001, Delanoë's first act against the tyranny of the automobile was to institute Paris Plage in the summer, closing the riverside expressways to cars during July and allowing pedestrians, bikes and tourists to colonize the *boules* pitches, cafés and other attractions that sprang up in their stead. Fast forward to 2013, and large parts of the Seine's banks are being made more cycle-friendly. On the Rive Gauche, the road between the Musée d'Orsay and the Pont de l'Alma has been shut, creating a promised 4.5 hectares (9.8 acres) of new floating gardens, trees and sports grounds. And on the opposite site of the river, the *voie rapide*, so beloved of Parisian motorists, has been slowed with traffic lights and narrowed to make more space for cycle lanes and pavements.

Delanoë's biggest achievement, however, is surely the Vélib, the municipal bike-hire scheme introduced in 2007. Though it has its drawbacks, the Vélib has humanized Paris's roads and made cycling an everyday activity, which everyone from businessmen to *bobo* hipsters, chic fashionistas to *mamies* (grannies), uses to go about their daily life; see Essential Bike Info (p. 44) for more on how to use it. Once you've found a decent Vélib, the city is yours to explore at your leisure. Paris is a compact place – the *Périphérique*, that fearsome, traffic-snarled ring road cutting Paris off from its suburbs, is only 35km (22 miles) in circumference – but extremely dense, which has consequences for the two-wheeled. It will take you quite a while to get anywhere; the city can be congested, and you will be stopping frequently at traffic lights. Pay good attention to the typical journey times indicated on our maps. Unless you know exactly where you're going, the labyrinthine layout and small, one-way streets rarely make cutting through the backstreets the swiftest option. Stick to the major roads with bike lanes if you're in a hurry to get somewhere.

The upside, however, of the amazing density to life in Paris is that there's so much to see, do, smell and eat. We've suggested five neighbourhoods to explore, but have barely touched on the *Quartier Latin*; we haven't taken you to the Palais de Tokyo or the Eiffel Tower, Montparnasse or the village-like Butte aux Cailles. So hop on your Vélib, and get out there and explore.

NEIGHBOURHOODS

LOUVRE, LES HALLES

THE CITY OF LIGHTS

We'll start our bicycle tour of Paris's beautiful, historic, culture-filled centre on the *parvis* outside **Notre Dame** ①. Why? Because it's the 'zero kilometre' from which French road signs are measured. And, although you could while the day away simply watching the river, sitting on the *quais* under the willow trees on the end of the **Île de la Cité** ②, there are world-class museums, shops and restaurants to explore. We're concentrating on the chic shopping district around the <u>rue St-Honoré</u>, and the trendier area of Montorgeuil, centred on the <u>rue Étienne Marcel</u> and <u>rue Tiquetonne</u>.

First stop, the **Jeu de Paume** ③, France's national centre of photography. Set in the genteel **Jardin des Tuileries** ④, it excels in exhibitions that span from the birth of the medium to the present day. To the east, **Maison Francis Kurkdjian** ⑤, the eponymous perfume boutique from the 'nose' behind such names as Dior and Guerlain, will get you in the spirit of the area. It sells elegant unisex fragrances, scented laundry detergent and even bubble blowers. The boutique is just off the rue St-Honoré, one of Paris's premier streets for luxury shops and the sort of hotels you might expect to see paparazzi outside. Here you'll find **Boutique LOOK** ⑥, where the French bicycle maker sells its recently revived upmarket clothing range; you may even see one of its Mondrian-influenced bikes, too. It's not far from **Colette** ⑦, the city's original concept store, where men's and women's prêt-a-porter sits next to books, magazines and designer bits and bobs, all policed by achingly cool shop assistants.

Take a little spin around the grand <u>place Vendôme</u> ⑧ before heading further along to **Astier de Villatte** ⑨, which sells its own charming, coveted earthenware, just opposite **Cafés Verlet** ⑩, a century-old purveyor of deliciously aromatic roasts of single-origin beans and house blends. Stop off in the salon for a cup and some accompanying cake before visiting the **place du Marché St-Honoré** ⑪ for more luxury shops, this time ranged around a former convent-turned-car park, which was rescued and renovated by architect Ricardo Bofill in 1996. It's now a monumental glass-roofed hall. Just to the south, architect Jean Nouvel has also been at work, on the wing of the Louvre that houses the **Musée des Arts Décoratifs** ⑫. Exhibits include rooms from Jeanne Lanvin's Art Deco apartment and classic pieces of modern furniture.

Now we're heading over towards the Montorgeuil area; the roads squeezing between its grand buildings are pretty congested, but there is a good – and improving – network of cycle lanes that will keep you away from the traffic. In the centre of town, especially, it's good to pay attention to the cycle lanes, and stick to them where you can. Taking a little detour for some food, however, is allowed. Try **Téléscope** ⑬ for serious coffee and cake, and **Claus** ⑭, a two-storey eatery full of groceries downstairs and healthy, German-inflected dishes up. **Café Noir** ⑮, meanwhile, is a retro-furnished corner café with old-school red banquettes that's charmingly rough around the edges. In these parts you'll find hip streetwear boutiques such as **Espace Kiliwatch** ⑯, one of the pioneers of the rue Étienne-Marcel, which sells hip denim and footwear brands and casual shirts. Down the rue Tiquetonne, which has a similar vibe, **En Selle Marcel** ⑰ is a chic bike shop full of beautiful bikes and accessories, with staff who will also repair your steed. The **passage du Grand Cerf** ⑱, meanwhile, is a classic, covered shopping arcade, with beautiful wooden façades and huge windows, which a range of quirky small boutiques call home.

Towards the end of the day, we recommend steering clear of Les Halles, but heading up towards the Faubourg St-Denis is a good bet. **Frenchie Wine Bar** ⑲ is the busy younger sister to the much-lauded restaurant opposite, while the **Experimental Cocktail Club** ⑳ is a

speakeasy-style bar that serves expertly mixed cocktails, attracting a chic crowd for late-night high jinks, particularly during fashion week. Or, as the day ends, head to the Tuileries, grab one of the reclining chairs in fashionable municipal green, and watch the sun go down.

REFUELLING

FOOD
Collette's basement restaurant, the **Water Bar** ㉑, is a good lunch spot **Stohrer** ㉒, established in 1730, is the city's oldest *pâtisserie*

DRINK
Join Parisians and tourists alike and buy a good bottle of wine to enjoy al fresco on the **Pont des Arts** ㉓ as the sun goes down over the most romantic city in the world

WI-FI
The **Café des Initiés** ㉔ is *branché* – well connected – in more ways than one

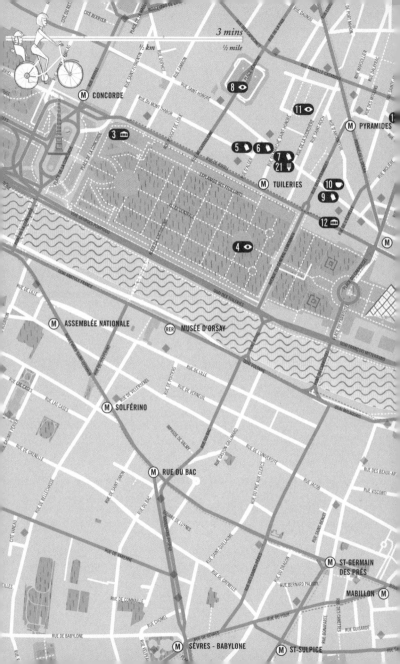

MARTYRS, PIGALLE, MONTMARTRE

BOHEMIAN DELIGHTS
AND TOURIST SIGHTS

The martyred St Denis, Bishop of Paris in the third century, has given his name to a few places around the city, including the rue des Martyrs in the 9th arrondissement, which commemorates his 10km (6-mile) walk, holding his severed head, after his beheading at the top of Montmartre. You won't find him at the basilica of **Sacré Cœur** ①, which occupies the spot now but was only completed in 1914. St Denis's statue is at Notre Dame (p. 11), and there's a basilica dedicated to him in the Paris suburb of St Denis, where he is supposed to have walked, preaching a sermon, following his execution. (You can ride there by following our Day On The Bike route to La Villette, then taking the left-hand fork of the canal.)

The neighbourhood we're exploring here extends west to the place de Clichy and east almost to the rue de Clignancourt. Don't head up to the iconic, picturesque Montmartre without stopping on the way to experience the 'bobo' (*bourgeois-bohème*) rue des Martyrs in the south, which has a village-like feel. You'll want to stop anyway, since the rue des Martyrs is where the streets tip towards the sky – head north towards Montmartre and all the roads will climb considerably. They're perfectly possible to ride up if you're feeling enthusiastic; you may want to think twice if you're on a Vélib, however, or take lots of breaks. Try *pâtissier* and ice-cream maker **Sébastien Gaudard** ② for sweet treats, or the stylish **Rose Bakery** ③ for coffee, cool drinks and delectable English-inspired bakes. Cut to the left to visit **Le Rocketship** ④, a neighbourhood café and design gift shop, and, even further west near the place de Clichy, the happening **Le Bal** ⑤, tucked away in a mews. Le Bal is an independent exhibition space in a former ballroom, dedicated to photography and new media, and also has a great bookshop and café.

For more traditional arts and culture, try the **Musée de la Vie Romantique** ⑥, a pretty house on a courtyard now filled with furniture and artefacts from the Romantic period, as well as memorabilia from writer Georges Sand and an adorable café in the conservatory. If, however, you stay on the rue des Martyrs, you'll find some quality *brocantes* (antiques shops), including **Et Puis C'est Tout** ⑦ and **L'Objet Qui Parle** ⑧, which straddle the louche boulevards around Pigalle, the historic centre of Paris's red-light district. Nearby, the **Galerie Christine Diegoni** ⑨ specializes in modern design, with furniture, lighting and objets d'art from George Nelson, Charles and Ray Eames, and Jean Prouvé in its collection. It's for window shopping only, unless you've got a very understanding bank manager.

North of Pigalle, the upper reaches of the rue des Martyrs begin to feel a bit more bohemian – you'll find the contemporary art gallery **Papier Peints** ⑩ here – and the road keeps heading up, getting ever steeper. You'll begin to see the staircases that Montmartre is so famous for, with pedestrians streaming up and down the hill. If you're thirsty, stop in the picturesque **place des Abbesses** ⑪, at one of Paris's 120 'Wallace fountains'. Built in the nineteenth century thanks to a well-meaning Brit, Sir Richard Wallace, to provide drinking water for all, they're recognizable by their glossy paint and sculpted caryatids, and have become an icon of the city. Alternatively, try the **Café des Deux Moulins** ⑫, the traditional café that starred in the international hit film *Amélie*, or **Boulangerie Gontran Cherrier** ⑬, a modern French baker known for his coloured breads and tasty sandwiches.

Above Abbesses, the roads fill with tourists, to the point where you may have to get off and walk. If you've made it up here, congratulations – the views are worth it, and there's always something

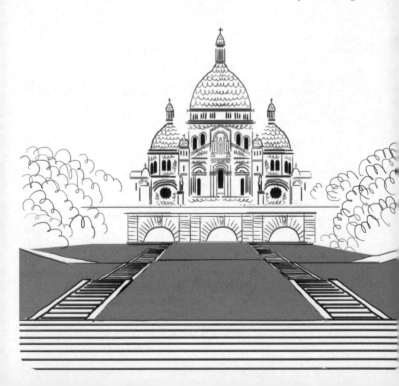

interesting going on for the myriad tourists who make the climb. Freewheel down the other side of the hill, and you'll spot the **Clos Montmartre vineyard** ⑭, source of its highly prized wine (if only for the labels painted by local artists), which is auctioned for charity each year. For something stronger, head to **Le Carmen** ⑮, a shabby-chic cocktail bar in a grand old house that was once home to the nineteenth-century composer, Georges Bizet.

REFUELLING

FOOD	DRINK
Bistrot des Dames ⑯ for classic dishes, al fresco	**La Fourmi** ⑱ is a good spot to catch a cold drink in the summer sun
Hôtel Amour ⑰ – cocktails and comfort food in this vintage-cool boutique hotel	**Au Rêve** ⑲ is a cute little place on the north side of the hill

WI-FI
Black Market ⑳ is a great *café freelance*, with artisan-made coffee, cheesecake and free Wi-Fi

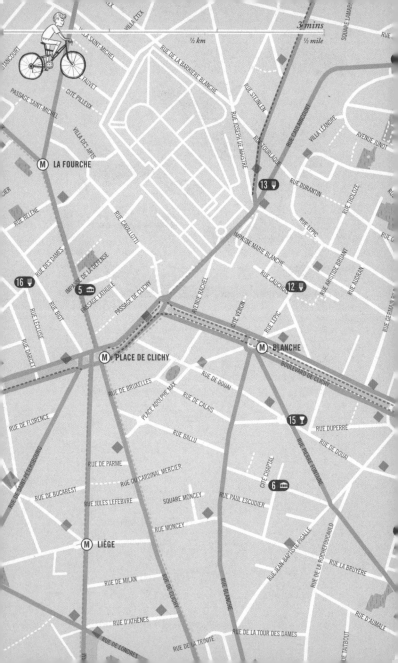

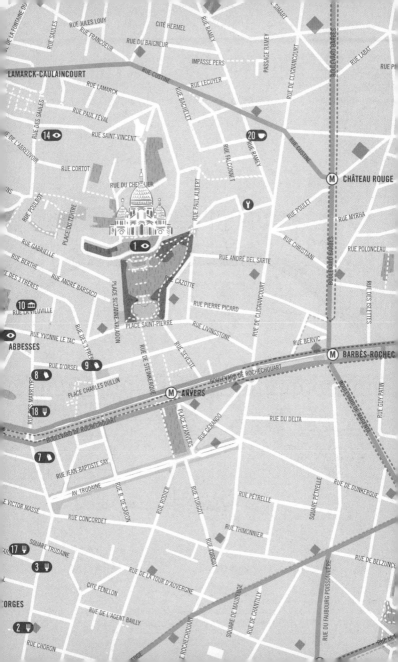

The Canal St-Martin's tranquil waters and elegant ironwork have been celebrated both in paint (by the Impressionist artist Alfred Sisley) and in film (in Marcel Carné's *Hôtel du Nord*). The **hotel** ① still stands – an authentic slice of old-school Paris, with a restaurant and zinc-topped bar looking out through thick velvet curtains to the canal. There's a terrace for sunny days, and 10 bikes available, free of charge, for guests. It's a perfect launchpad for exploring the area, which lies west of the restaurants and bars of the rue du Faubourg St-Denis and east of the edgy nightlife of Belleville. Visit on a cloudy Monday morning and the neighbourhood will be deserted, relaxed to the point of being horizontal; come back on a sunny Saturday afternoon, however, and every inch of available space next to the water will have been filled by the hip locals.

Today the southern section of the canal, which was constructed by Napoleon to provide fresh water to Paris's teeming masses, has been paved over, forcing the water under gardens, playgrounds and parks. In the north, it joins the Canal de l'Ourcq at the <u>place de la Bataille-de-Stalingrad</u>, very close to **Point Éphémère** ②, which hosts concerts, DJ events and exhibitions from emerging artists; on summer evenings, the crowds spill out on to the quayside. But if you're travelling up from Bastille, the first spot you'll hit is **Chez Prune** ③, a local institution that's great for daytime drinks, a quick bite or late-night beer and wine, cosied up inside or on the outdoor terrace. It's on the corner of the <u>rue de Marseille</u>, which, along with the <u>rues Toudic</u> and <u>Beaurepaire</u>, are the shopping heart of the district, with fashion boutiques and design pop-ups. Parisian contemporary clothing brand **APC** ④ is here (its original store is in the 5th) as is, on the same stretch, **Centre Commercial** ⑤, an eco-friendly concept store that stocks clothes and shoes from stylish independent brands, organic beauty products, second-hand bikes and vintage furniture.

Up the road are two stand-out bookshops: **Artazart** ⑥, for architecture, art and design books; and **Le 29** ⑦, a photography bookshop with exhibition space and a DIY print lab upstairs. Le 29 is on the <u>rue des Récollets</u>, a street that is typical of the area's charm, with artsy boutiques, good restaurants and the pretty **Jardin Villemin** ⑧. Here, too, in a former convent is the **Maison de l'architecture en Île-de-France** ⑨, an architectural association that organizes temporary exhibitions and an annual festival. But the main draw for initiated

is the Maison's Café A, hidden away in an idyllic, tree-lined court-yard, just steps away from the bustle of the Gare de l'Est.

If you're in need of refreshment, **Du Pain et des Idées** ⑩ is an old-style *boulangerie* run by an award-winning baker; also nicely traditional is **Le Petit Chateau d'Eau** ⑪, all flowery wallpaper, leather banquettes, coffee and unpretentious food. Or, for some-thing more up-to-date, **Café Craft** ⑫ is one of the new breed of coffee-chic cafés that are springing up in the trendier areas, catering to the laptop-happy freelancers now colonizing the French capital. Alternatively, head to the hilly, romantic **Parc des Buttes Chaumont** ⑬, and do not neglect **Le siège du Parti communiste français** ⑭ on your way past; the Communist Party HQ was designed by archi-tect Oscar Niemeyer, and combines an undulating glazed building with a white dome that conceals futuristic underground debating chambers. To finish the day, the agreeably chaotic **Aux Deux Amis** ⑮ (just off-map, on the rue Oberkampf) does inventive small plates of food, along with cold beer on tap and good wine too.

REFUELLING

FOOD
Castro & Co ⑯ is a brilliant deli with Turkish and Middle Eastern food
Verbano Traiteur ⑰ for similar Mediterranean treats

DRINK
Le Carillon ⑱, next to the canal, is perfect for a sundowner apéritif

WI-FI
Rosa Bonheur ⑲ in the Parc des Buttes Chaumont will connect you to the net

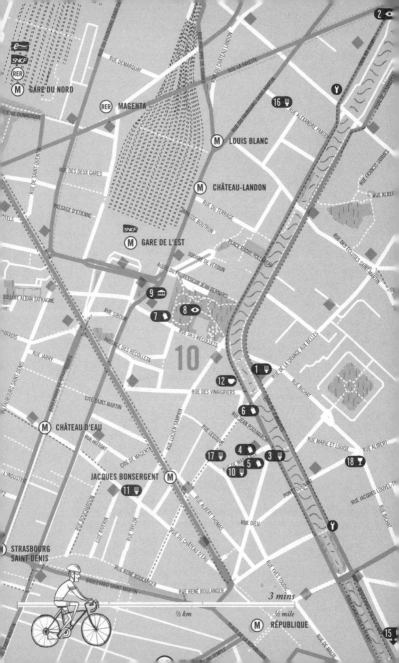

10

GARE DU NORD

RER **MAGENTA**

M **LOUIS BLANC**

M **CHÂTEAU-LANDON**

M **GARE DE L'EST**

M **CHÂTEAU D'EAU**

JACQUES BONSERGENT M

**STRASBOURG
SAINT-DENIS**

M **RÉPUBLIQUE**

16 🍴

9 🚋

7 ⚫   8 👁

1 🍴

12 💗

6 🍦

4 🍴   3 🍴

17 🍴   5 🍦

10 🍴

11 🍴

18 🍸

15

3 mins

½ km   ½ mile

The Marais sits on the Right Bank in the 4th arrondissement, east of Châtelet and Les Halles, and broadly north of the rue de Rivoli, behind the Hôtel de Ville and the Pompidou Centre. But whereas the southern Marais is very touristy and can feel slightly stuck up, the northern end is one of the most dynamic cultural areas in Paris, with contemporary art galleries, independent shops and cafés. We're talking the area west of the boulevard Beaumarchais, and north of the Rambuteau and Chemin Vert Métro stations. If you're cycling from the rue de Turbigo in the west, try heading in through the **passage de l'Ancre** ①, a hidden treasure. One of many such passages snaking between Paris's grand boulevards, this tranquil passageway is full of trees, flowers and greenery, as well as some special independent boutiques, including the city's only umbrella-repair shop. You'll feel a million miles away from the centre of a metropolis.

Just north is **La Gaîté Lyrique** ②, a digital-arts centre, which houses concerts and exhibitions over five floors; the bar, juxtaposing contemporary interior design and original nineteenth-century marble, is also impressive. Stop off at **Freemoos** ③, a cycling concept store a bit further on for city-specific bike bits, folding bikes and e-bikes. Staff will also repair your bike if there's something amiss, as will **Bicycle Store** ④, a top-of-the-range bike shop specializing in urban and street styles. The northern Marais is home to a thriving art scene, including independent bookshop **Øfr** ⑤. The brother and sister who run it maintain a back-room gallery, and there are also bags, accessories and shoes from independent designers. **Librairie Comme un roman** ⑥ is a more mainstream bookseller, yet still with a good selection of design, art and other unusual titles.

Straying into the southern Marais, the **Musée Picasso** ⑦ is a big tourist draw, but it's the independent galleries that really distinguish the area. **Galerie Yvon Lambert** ⑧ is run by Paris's original contemporary art gallerist, who since the 1960s has represented Nan Goldin, Jenny Holzer and Anselm Kiefer, among others; the bookshop next door, with its colour-coded bookshelves, is also worth a look. **Galerie Emmanuel Perrotin** ⑨ in the rue de Turenne, meanwhile, is among the most influential contemporary galleries worldwide, and **Galerie BSL** ⑩ in the rue Charlot presents a beautiful range of pieces of contemporary design. The street is also home to many smaller French designers – try **N°60** ⑪ for edgy men's and women's fashion, while **Les Fées** ⑫ has a carefully edited selection of homewares and fabrics.

Of course, the Haut Marais's temple to all things interior design is **Merci** ⑬, on the busy rue Beaumarchais. Enter through into the courtyard, past the scarlet Fiat 500, and a world of furniture, accessories and fashion awaits. It's a great place to browse, and the two cafés are a brilliant pit stop at any time of day. For some more recherché pieces, try **Lieu Commun** ⑭, owned by French designer Matali Crasset, a protégée of Philippe Starck.

When it comes to dining in the northern Marais, try **Nanashi** ⑮, which serves Japanese-influenced French food (think bento boxes and brioche pizzas), or any of the numerous stalls at the **Marché des Enfants Rouges** ⑯. Located on the fascinating rue de Bretagne, the market sells everything from charcuterie to sushi to Moroccan salads. For a treat, **La Chocolaterie de Jacques Génin** ⑰ looks more like a gallery than a chocolate shop, but really delivers the goods, and serves up arguably the city's best *millefeuille*. **Café Pinson** ⑱ does good veggie food, while **Chez Janou** ⑲ is a Provençal restaurant that's a favourite with locals and tourists (make sure you order the chocolate mousse for desert).

As the evening progresses, try **Le Progrès** ⑳, a quintessential Parisian bar-tobacconist that's also a lively meeting place for local fashionistas and arty types. Sit on the terrace, order a bottle of rosé and people-watch the night away.

REFUELLING

FOOD	DRINK
Breizh Café ㉑, because you couldn't leave France without eating crêpes	**Merce and the Muse** ㉓, an East Village-style coffee shop serving up good muffins
Mi-Va-Mi ㉒, in the south, for falafels	

WI-FI
La Terrasse des Archives ㉔ has a cosily enclosed terrace – the perfect place to fire off some emails

RUE SAINTE-FOY
RUE DU CAIRE
RUE D'ALEXANDRIE
SAINT-MARTIN
RUE MESLAY
RUE DU CAIRE
RUE NOTRE DAME DE
RUE DU VERTBOIS
RUE DU PONCEAU
2 🍸
Ⓜ RÉAUMUR – SÉBASTOPOL
RUE DUSSOUBS
RUE BORDA
Ⓜ ARTS ET MÉTIERS
RUE GRENETA
RUE CUNIN GRIDAINE
PASSAGE DU GRAND-CERF
RUE AU MAIRE
RUE DE TURBIGO
RUE DU TEMPLE
1 👁
RUE PASTOURELLE
Ⓜ ÉTIENNE MARCEL
3
RUE CHAPON
RUE DU CYGNE
RUE DE MONTMORENCY
3 🍸
BOULEVARD DE SÉBASTOPOL
RUE DU GRENIER SAINT-LAZARE
RUE RAMBUTEAU
IMPASSE BEAUBOURG
RUE SAINT-MARTIN
RUE RAMBUTEAU
RUE RAMBUTEAU
LLES
RUE RAMBUTEAU
Ⓜ RAMBUTEAU
24 ❤
RUE DES ARCHIVES
RUE DES QUATRE FI
CITÉ NOËL
RUE RAMBUTEAU
RUE DE LA REYNIE
RUE DES FRANCS BOURGEOIS
RUE SAINT-MERRI
RUE DES LOMBARDS
RUE DE PLÂTRE
RUE SAINT-BON
RUE DU RENARD
RUE SAINT-MERRI
RUE DU TEMPLE
RUE AUBRIOT
RUE DE LA VERRERIE
🍸
RUE DE MOUSSY
RUE COUTELLERIE
RUE VIEILLE DU TEMPLE
RUE DU TRÉSOR
22 🍴
Ⓜ HÔTEL DE VILLE
3 mins
RUE RUE DE RIVOLI
½ km
½ mile
RUE DU ROI DE SICILE
🍸

RIVE GAUCHE

OH-SO-CHIC SHOPPING AND GALLERIES

Paris's Left Bank has been traditionally known for its intellectual cafés, bookshops and jazz, its student rebellions and chic but bohemian living. The present-day Rive Gauche, which, broadly speaking, encompasses the 5th, 6th and 7th arrondissements (on what is actually the southern bank of the Seine), still resounds with all these associations. We're concentrating on the area north of the **Jardin du Luxembourg** ①, which, with its avenues of trees, metal chairs and old men playing chess, is Paris's most elegant park. It's just below the fashionable 6th, with its high-end shopping, and the more bustling side of the 7th. On the way through the Latin Quarter, however (so named because of the once-large numbers of Latin-speaking students at the Sorbonne), make sure to stop at **Shakespeare & Company** ②, the world-famous English-language bookshop. It's not the original shop, which gave succour to literary émigrés such as Hemingway and Pound, but this second edition still offers sleeping space to young writers and promotes an annual literary festival.

West across the boulevard St-Michel, the buildings get grander and the shopfronts more polished: you're entering St Germain-des-Prés, whose boutiques and galleries are a glimpse into a sophisticated, often expensive world. **Galerie Kreo** ③, for example, a stark white space that specializes in contemporary design, exhibits objets d'art and renowned names from the worlds of furniture and lighting. It's not far from **Cire Trudon** ④, candle-makers since 1643, which supplied the court at Versailles and, after relaunching in 2006, provided the candles for Sofia Coppola's film *Marie Antoinette*. The shop is at the bottom of the rue de Seine, behind **St-Sulpice** ⑤, the second-largest church in Paris, which presides over a pretty square. Further up is the junction with the rue de Buci, a lively street with a bustling *marché* ⑥ that you may have trouble squeezing down on your bike. No matter: take a breather at **Café Germain** ⑦, where designer India Mahdavi has created an Alice-in-Wonderland scene with chequered floors and a giant sculpture of a girl breaking through the ceiling. Close by, you'll find **Galerie Salon des Antiquités & Astier de Villate** ⑧, a shop full of antique curios and beautiful ceramics, and **Le Labo** ⑨. Founded by two Frenchmen, initially in New York, it's styled as an old-fashioned apothecary, making perfumes to order while you wait.

Continue west and you'll find **La Hune** ⑩, the most important of the Rive Gauche bookshops, which recently moved into bright new premises in which to display its art, fashion and design books. It has a great stationery department, too. La Hune is opposite the

Magnum Gallery ⑪, the Paris HQ of the Magnum photographic co-operative. It hosts two annual exhibitions, with limited-edition prints and signed publications for sale. Just round the corner is **Peterhof** ⑫, a specialist in all things Russian, including dolls. It must have the most enchanting shop window in a city of enchanting shop windows. If luxury fashion is your thing, the busy <u>boulevard St-Germain</u> and roads around the <u>rue Bonaparte</u> will slake your thirst for the big brands, and **Hermès** ⑬ is definitely worth visiting. The mosaic-tiled former Art Deco swimming pool accommodates a bookstore and tea room, with goods displayed under 9m (30-ft) high wooden huts. **Pierre Hermé** ⑭ is one of the two big Parisian names in macaroons; his culinary creations create queues into the street. Try the outlandish strawberry and wasabi, or traditional salted caramel.

Heading ever westwards, cycle down the <u>rue de l'Université</u>, checking out the long-established antiques shops, full of amazing items and curiosities (but probably twice the price of the already expensive flea markets), and head into **Deyrolle** ⑮, an eccentric Left Bank institution. Downstairs is gardening gear, while upstairs are an unmissable wood-panelled taxidermy workshop and show-room that feels more like a museum. Next door is **Galerie Maeght** ⑯. Originally established on the Côte d'Azur, it wowed Paris with its inaugural exhibition in 1945, featuring the work of Henri Matisse.

The gallery has since displayed some of the biggest names in modern art, but also sells surprisingly inexpensive prints.

Just off-map, down the rue de Varenne, is the **Musée Rodin** ⑰, an expansive villa and garden full of the master's sculptures in bronze. Before you venture off, however, stop for a drink at **Café le Basile** ⑱, full of *Nouvelle Vague* style and students and profs from the prestigious Sciences Po university nearby. Alternatively, head to **Coutume Café** ⑲ (off-map, on rue de Babylone), which is perhaps the godfather of the burgeoning Paris coffee scene. It also does a great brunch at the weekend.

REFUELLING

FOOD
La Pâtisserie des Rêves ⑳, for excellent pastries and takeaway hot chocolate
Fish La Boissonerie ㉑, in a former fishmongers, for light, healthy food and good wine

DRINK
La Dernière Goutte ㉒ is a wine bar with Left Bank style

WI-FI
Café le Buci ㉓ is perfect for catching up on emails and watching the world go by

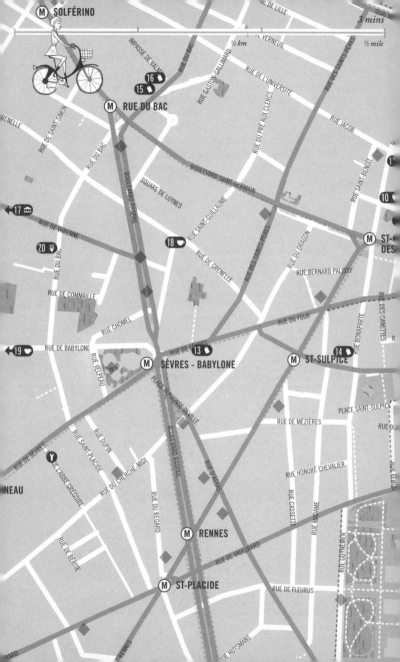

RACING AND TRAINING

On 7 November 1869, the world's first-ever bicycle road race set off from Paris for Rouen. Almost eleven hours later an Englishman, James Moore, won, inaugurating an era of cycle sport that still has Paris at its centre. Paris–Rouen was followed by numerous other races similarly started as publicity stunts for sports newspapers, including Bordeaux–Paris and Paris–Brest–Paris in 1891, and Paris–Roubaix in 1896. Then in 1902, a junior reporter at *L'Auto* suggested staging a race around France to revive the ailing paper's fortunes, and the following year the Tour de France was born. The first Tour set off from **Le Réveil Matin**, a bar in the southern suburb of Montgeron, and ended at the Parc des Princes velodrome, in Paris, some 2,500km (1,500 miles) later. It was won by Maurice Garin, one of the favourites, who finished more than 65 hours ahead of the last-placed man.

Since then, the Tour has always finished in Paris, though it wasn't until 1975 that the Champs-Elysées sprint was introduced. Paris–Roubaix, one of the fixtures of the cycling calendar, still lives on, as does Paris–Brest–Paris: the 1,200km (746-mile) out-and-back is no longer raced but held as an endurance brevet, with the self-sufficient participants given a time limit of ninety hours to complete the course. Bordeaux–Paris, which in later years was motor-paced (riders sheltered from the wind behind motorbikes), was last run in 1988, but many other races between the capital to provincial towns remain: Paris–Nice, a week-long stage race, which takes place in March; Paris–Tours, held in the autumn, the most prominent of the one-day races; as well as Paris–Camembert, Paris–Bourges, and many more. But be warned: only the Tour actually heads into central Paris. The rest start in Paris's sprawling suburbs or in the surrounding Île-de-France region.

Unsurprisingly, many of France's greatest cyclists have lived in and around the capital. In the early days, there were Octave Lapize, the first man to climb the legendary Col de Tourmalet in the Tour de France, and the famously unlucky Eugène Christophe, the first wearer of the yellow jersey in 1919. He never won the Tour, and was hampered by mechanical problems: twice he had to weld his forks mid-race. The famed Pélissier brothers (three brothers – Henri, Francis and Charles – who all raced in the early part of the twentieth

century) settled in Paris, though they were originally from Auvergne. In more recent times, the two-time Tour winner in the 1980s, Laurent Fignon (nicknamed 'Le Prof' for his reflective nature and round spectacles), was born in Montmartre, though his family soon moved into the Île-de-France. These days, David Moncoutié, Sandy Casar, Tony Gallopin and Yoann Offredo are all associated with the Paris region. Cyclists in the area are blessed with many great clubs, which feed the world's top cycling teams. Fignon was a member of US Créteil, while Athletic Club de Boulogne-Billancourt has helped big names, including André Darrigade, Jean Stablinski, Stephen Roche and Robert Millar, find their professional legs.

Although Paris doesn't currently have a top-level track, in the old days there were several: **Parc des Princes** (now a football, rugby and concert venue) was originally a velodrome, while the Vélodrome d'Hiver ('winter velodrome') was the first permanent indoor track in France. Both were built by Henri Desgrange, the founder of the Tour de France. He had become a convert to cycle racing, watching the finish of the first Bordeaux–Paris race at the velodrome at the Porte Maillot. In those days it was usual for road races to finish with a few laps of the track (mostly as a money-making wheeze for the track owners), and the young Desgrange was transfixed. He took up the sport straight away, and set many time-trial records for cycling at different distances. You'll still see some *pistards* in Paris: France's national elite sporting academy, **L'Insep,** is in the Bois de Vincennes. It has a private indoor track, but if you're lucky, you'll see track stars like Grégory Baugé and Michaël D'Almeida warming down in the *bois*, or at the **Vélodrome Jacques Anquetil,** named after the five-time Tour winner. The Bois de Vincennes is also a meeting spot for the capital's road cyclists: in the eastern corner is a triangular circuit, where many come to let off steam. (For more on the *bois*, see our A Day On The Bike section.) The **Hippodrome de Longchamp,** however, in the western Bois de Boulogne is where you'll find a faster ride. For links to these spots, and to racing and training routes, head to the Links and Addresses section.

If you need spares or repairs for your road bike, **Cycles Laurent, Cycles St-Honoré** and the **Paris Bike Co.** will look after you well. If you own a Giant, there's a **Giant Store** in the centre, and, for all things related to touring bikes, Paris's specialist is **Rando Cycles.** For hiring options, check Essential Bike Info (p. 44).

ESSENTIAL BIKE INFO

Paris is a compact city that, though hectic, is great fun to cycle around. Here are some tips for hassle-free pedalling.

ETIQUETTE

Compared with some northern European cities, Paris's roads are a bit of a free-for-all, though there are a couple of things you should know:

- Parisians mainly ride where they're meant to, but you will see bikes on pavements and all over the place. If you are going off-piste, make sure it's safe.
- At some traffic lights in France, it's now OK to turn right on a bike on a red. Many people will turn right on red lights, even where it's not sanctioned, but exercise your discretion.

SAFETY

Keep your eyes open, and you'll have fun. Here are a few pointers:

- Avoid big roads without bike lanes in rush hour, as they can become manic. And the big gyratories – the Arc de Triomphe, Bastille and Concorde, for example – are only for the hardy at any time. Check our 'roads to avoid' on the maps for a guide to some places to exercise extra caution.
- Remember, if you're uncertain about a junction, you can always dismount and cross with the pedestrians.
- Even when on a bike lane, you may get cars turning your way, or pedestrians ambling into your path. The bike lanes are making a great improvement to cycling in the city, but Parisian drivers are more assertive, and less aware, than in Holland or Belgium.
- Give way to the right. On French roads, unless signposted differently, traffic from the right has priority – even when it seems like it's coming from a minor road.
- Be careful at big junctions, because two separate streams of traffic sometimes filter at once.
- Beware the contraflow bike lane. This relatively new invention is indicated on one-way streets by road markings and the words *sauf vélo* ('bicycles excepted') under the no-entry sign. Unfortunately, Parisian drivers are usually unaware of your right to travel in the opposite direction to them, and won't make allowances for you. Many of these streets are very narrow.

- People park cars everywhere! Keep an eye out for cars perched on the pavement at junctions or making double-parking manoeuvres.
- Compared with other cities (like London, for example), the Parisian traffic has fewer large vehicles and lorries, making visibility quite good, but beware of bendy buses nevertheless.

SECURITY

Paris does not seem to be quite as much a thieves' paradise as some cities. However, common sense applies. Do not leave any bike unlocked and unattended, and take your cues from local cyclists: if you don't see any bikes locked in a certain area, then it's probably not a good idea to leave yours either. If you've brought a valuable bike to town, always lock it with a good lock to a bike rack or lamp-post, or some other immovable thing. Think about using two locks, so that opportunist bike thieves will pick an easier target.

FINDING YOUR WAY

Paris's bike routes have a network of small green signposts to direct you to major destinations. These are generally good, and won't leave you directionless too often. The signs for car traffic on major roads are useful, too, so if you've even a vague idea of the city's layout, you'll be able to keep heading in the right direction. Bus stops also have useful maps. Many people refer to destinations by their *arrondissement*, the different administrative sectors of Paris. Numbered 1 to 19, they spiral out, like a snail's shell, clockwise from the middle. The Eiffel Tower is in the 7th, many of the cool bars in the 11th, and so on.

VÉLIBS AND BIKE HIRE

When the **Vélib** (the name is formed from the words *vélo*, meaning bicycle, and *liberté*, or freedom) was introduced in 2007, it put Paris at the forefront of a city-cycling revolution. Over 7,000 bicycles were distributed across 750 stations throughout town. After the initial success, the number of bikes has been increased, so you're never more than around 300m (984 ft) from a docking station. Vélib now even extends to just outside the *Périphérique*.

The scheme is very well used, and has been, to some extent, a victim of its own success. In some areas (around Belleville, for example, and in the trendy eastern quarters), it's difficult to get a bike on a Sunday, since the stands are often emptied by Saturday-night revellers. And in the residential suburbs, docking stations can become full after the evening commute – which can be a problem if you're trying to dock near the edge of the zone. There's not much you can do in these cases, other than be wise to the fact it may happen. The computer terminals at the docking stations will help you find alternative parking places, and there are mobile apps available to help you plan your journey from one station to another, and show you the available bikes and free spaces at each one. What's worse is that, more than in any other city, the stations seem to be heavily populated with broken or unroadworthy bikes. Any bike with a back-to-front saddle has been set that way by a user, to alert the maintenance crews and other cyclists. Before you commit to a particular bike make sure you test the brakes, check the tyres aren't flat and that there isn't more serious damage (to the cranks or pedals, for example).

It's easy to sign up to Vélib online, or at the docking stations: all you need is a credit card, and after a simple sign-up, you'll be given a user number and PIN (write it down from the web, or take a print-out from the docking terminal). Follow the on-screen instructions, choose a bike and you're off. Access costs €1.70 for a day or €8 for the week, and for this you get the first half an hour of each trip for free. Ride longer than that and you'll be charged €1 for the next half hour and an escalating price for longer periods. The idea is that you take the Vélib for a short journey and then dock it, to keep it in circulation. (The Vélibs do, however, have a kick-stand and chain lock, and it's common to see them parked on the streets.) If you want to dock your bike and the station is full, press a button and you'll be given 15 minutes free to find another station. Vélib stations above 60m (197 ft) in altitude are known as V+. If you dock a bike at a V+ station, you'll have 15 minutes taken off your time, as a reward for slogging up the hill. If your journey has been free anyway, this will be saved up for the next time you're charged.

For all its flaws (and the dreadful beige colour of the bikes themselves, which make the docking stations surprisingly hard to spot in the urban landscape), the Vélib scheme is convenient and easy to use. It's our recommendation for everyday city riding. The bikes are relatively speedy and good fun, but if you want to rent something more stylish, try **Gépetto & Vélos** in the 5th arrondissement. **Paris Cycles**, next to the Bois de Boulogne, will rent you a bike for some woodland cruising, and **Cycles Laurent** or the **Paris Bike Co.** will supply high-end road bikes for some real out-of-town exploring.

OTHER PUBLIC TRANSPORT

Bikes aren't allowed on Paris's buses and trams, or on the funicular to Montmartre. Nor are they allowed on the **Métro**, except on line 1, on Sundays and public holidays, when you can ask the station staff to let you through the barriers and wheel your bike on.

On the **RER**, Paris's light-rail system, bicycles are only allowed on trains outside the rush hour – that's all weekend and not between 6:30 and 9am or 4:30 and 7pm on weekdays.

TRAVELLING TO PARIS WITH BIKES

Paris is easily reached by national and international train services, which are the safest way to travel with a bike. If you're coming from the UK, **Eurostar** will take bicycles on its services but, unfortunately, from 2013, only folding bikes in bags less than 85cm (33 in.) in length can be taken as carry-on luggage onto the trains. Instead, you must either book it a place (currently £30 per journey; it will be hung on a hook in the goods van), or put it in a bag and send it via the registered baggage service. The 'Turn Up and Go' option, where you leave your bike bag at a counter in the check-in hall, costs £10 each way.

On the high-speed **TGV** and **Thalys** trains, which connect Paris to Belgium, Amsterdam, Geneva, Cologne and on down to Spain and Italy, a bagged bike can be carried for free. The large luggage racks make the whole business fairly hassle-free. Two strategies seem to work: either race to the front of the queue, so that you can be sure of securing the space you want in the rack; or, if your bike bag is fairly slimline, wait until everyone else has stowed their stuff, and slide it in on top. German high-speed **ICE** trains will not allow bike bags longer than 85cm (33 in.), which practically rules out any non-folding bikes. Slower Intercity and Eurocity (**IC** and **EC**) trains allow bikes to be wheeled on board if you pay for a reservation, so factor in a non high-speed train if you're arriving in Paris from Germany.

Paris's airports are a long way from the centre of town, and stuck in a spaghetti junction of major traffic-filled roads, so cycling to and from your flight is not advised. Take public transport in to town instead.

LINKS AND ADDRESSES

Øfr
20, rue Dupetit-Thouars, 75003
ofrsystem.com

APC
5, rue de Marseille, 75010
apc.fr

Artazart
83, quai de Valmy, 75010
artazart.com

Astier de Villatte
173, rue St-Honoré, 75001
astierdevillatte.com

Au Rêve
89, rue Caulaincourt, 75018

Aux Deux Amis
45, rue Oberkampf, 75011

Aux Folies
8, rue de Belleville, 75020

Bar Ourcq
68 Quai de la Loire, 75019
barourcq.free.fr

Batofar
Port de la Gare, 75013
batofar.org

Bibliothèque Nationale de France
11, quai François Mauriac, 75013
bnf.fr

Bistrot des Dames
18, rue des Dames, 75017
eldoradohotel.fr

Bistrot du Peintre
116, avenue Ledru Rollin, 75011
bistrotdupeintre.com

Bistrot Paul Bert
20, rue Paul Bert,
93400 St-Ouen

Black Market
27, rue Ramey, 75018

Bois de Vincennes
Avenue de Gravelle,
94220 Charenton-le-Pont

Boulangerie Gontran Cherrier
22, rue Caulaincourt, 75018
gontrancherrierboulanger.com

Boutique LOOK
217, rue St-Honoré 75001
look-collection.com

Breizh Café
109, rue Vieille du Temple, 75003
breizhcafe.com

Café Craft
24, rue des Vinaigriers, 75010
cafe-craft.com

Café des Deux Moulins
15, rue Lepic, 75018

Café des Initiés
3, place des 2 Écus, 75001
lecafedesinities.com

Café Germain
25, rue de Buci, 75006

Café le Basile
34, rue de Grenelle, 75007
cafe-le-basile.com

Café le Buci
52, rue Dauphine, 75006
le-buci.com

Café Noir
15, rue St-Blaise, 75020
cafenoirparis.fr

Café Pinson
6, rue du Forez, 75003
cafepinson.fr

Cafés Verlet
256, rue St-Honoré, 75001
cafesverlet.com

Castro & Co
15b, rue Alexandre Parodi, 75010

Centre Commercial
2, rue de Marseille, 75010
centrecommercial.cc

Chez Janou
2, rue Roger Verlomme, 75003
chezjanou.com

Chez Prune
36, rue Beaurepaire, 75010

Cire Trudon
78, rue de Seine, 75006
ciretrudon.com

Claus
14, rue Jean-Jacques Rousseau,
75001
clausparis.com

Clos Montmartre vineyard
14–18, rue des Saules, 75018

Colette
213, rue St-Honoré 75001
colette.fr

Coulée Verte
Quinze-Vingts, 75012
promenade-plantee.org

Coutume Café
47, rue de Babylone, 75007
coutumecafe.com

Deyrolle
46, rue du Bac, 75007
deyrolle.com

Du Pain et des Idées
34, rue Yves Toudic, 75010
dupainetdesidees.com

Espace Kiliwatch
64, rue Tiquetonne, 75002
espacekiliwatch.fr

Et Puis C'est Tout
72, rue des Martyrs, 75009

Experimental Cocktail Club
37, rue St-Sauveur, 75002
experimentalcocktailclub.com

Fish La Boissonnerie
69, rue de Seine, 75006

Frenchie Wine Bar
5–6, rue du Nil, 75002
frenchie-restaurant.com

Galerie BSL
23, rue Charlot, 75003
galeriebsl.com

Galerie Christine Diegoni
47 ter, rue Orsel, 75018
christinediegoni.fr

Galerie Emmanuel Perrotin
76, rue de Turenne, 75003
perrotin.com

Galerie Kreo
31, rue Dauphine, 75006
galeriekreo.com

Galerie Maeght
42, rue du Bac, 75007
maeght.com/galeries

Galerie Salon Antiquités & Astier de Villatte
4, rue de Bourbon le Château,
75006
galeriesalon.blogspot.com

Galerie Yvon Lambert
108, rue Vieille du Temple 75003
yvon-lambert.com

Hermès
17, rue de Sèvres, 75006
hermes.com

Hôtel Amour
8, rue de Navarin, 75009
hotelamourparis.fr

Hôtel du Nord
102, quai de Jemmapes, 75010
hoteldunord.org

Institut du Monde Arabe
1, rue des Fossés St-Bernard,
75005
imarabe.org

Jardin des Plantes
57, rue Cuvier, 75005
jardindesplantes.net

Jardin des Tuileries
Place de la Concorde, 75001
louvre.fr

Jardin Villemin
14, rue des Récollets, 75010
paris.fr

Jeu de Paume
1, place de la Concorde, 75008
jeudepaume.org

La Chocolaterie de Jacques Genin
133, rue de Turenne, 75003
jacquesgenin.fr

La Dernière Goutte
6, rue de Bourbon le Château,
75006
ladernieregoutte.net

La Fourmi
74, rue des Martyrs, 75018

La Gaîté Lyrique
3 bis, rue Papin, 75003
gaite-lyrique.net

La Hune
16–18, ue de l'Abbaye, 75006

La Pâtisserie des Rêves
93, rue du Bac, 75007
lapatisseriedesreves.com

La Terrasse des Archives
51, rue des Archives, 75003

Le Bal
6, Impasse de la Défense, 75018
le-bal.fr

Le Baron Rouge
1, rue Théophile Roussel, 75012

Le Carillon
18, rue Alibert, 75010

Le Carmen
34, rue Duperré, 75009
le-carmen.fr

Le Labo
6, rue de Bourbon le Château,
75006
lelabofragrances.com

Le Petit Château d'Eau
34, rue du Château d'Eau, 75010

Le Progrès
1, rue de Bretagne, 75003

Le Réveil Matin
22, avenue Jean Jaurès,
91230 Montgeron
hotelreveilmatin.fr

Le Rocketship
13 bis, rue Henry Monnier,
75009
lerocketship.com

Les Docks: Cité de la Mode et du Design
34, quai d'Austerlitz, 75013
paris-docks-en-seine.fr

Les Fées
19, rue Charlot, 75003

Le siège du Parti communiste français
2, place du Colonel Fabien,
75019
pcf.fr

Le Trucmush
5, passage Thiéré, 75011
letrucmush.fr

Le 29
29, rue des Récollets, 75010
le29.fr

Librairie Comme un roman
39, rue de Bretagne, 75003
comme-un-roman.com

Lieu Commun
5, rue des Filles du Calvaire,
75003
lieucommun.fr

L'Objet Qui Parle
86, rue des Martyrs, 75018

Magnum Gallery
13, rue de l'Abbaye, 75006
magnumgallery.fr

Maison de l'architecture en Île-de-France
148 rue du Faubourg St-Martin,
75010
maisonarchitecture-idf.org

Maison Francis Kurkdjian
5, rue d'Alger, 75001
franciskurkdjian.com

Marché aux Puces St-Ouen
Porte de Clignancourt, 75018
marcheauxpuces-saintouen.com

Marché d'Aligre
Place d'Aligre, 75012
marchedaligre.free.fr

Marché Dauphine
134, rue des Rosiers,
93400 St-Ouen
marche-dauphine.com

Marché des Enfants Rouges
39, rue de Bretagne, 75003
egs-sa.com

Marché Rue de Buci
Rue de Buci, 75006

Marché Serpette
96–110, rue des Rosiers,
93400 St-Ouen
marcheserpette.com

Merce and the Muse
1 bis, rue Charles-François
Dupuis, 75003
merceandthemuse.com

Merci
111, boulevard Beaumarchais,
73003
merci-merci.com

Mi-Va-Mi
23, rue des Rosiers, 75004

Musée de la Vie Romantique
16, rue Chaptal, 75009
paris.fr

Musée des Arts Décoratifs
107, rue de Rivoli, 75001
lesartsdecoratifs.fr

Musée du Louvre
Musée du Louvre, 75001
louvre.fr

Musée Picasso
Rue de Thorigny, 75003
musee-picasso.fr

Musée Rodin
79, rue de Varenne, 75007
musee-rodin.fr

Nanashi
31, rue de Paradis, 75010
nanashi.fr

N°60
60, rue Charlot, 75003

Notre Dame
6 Parvis Notre-Dame,
Place Jean-Paul II, 75004
notredameparis.fr

Palais-Royal
Rue St-Honoré, 75001
paris.fr

Papiers Peints
11, rue la Vieuville, 75018
spree.fr

Parc des Buttes Chaumont
1, rue Botzaris, 75019
butteschaumont.free.fr

Passage du Grand Cerf
Passage du Grand Cerf, 75002
passagedugrandcerf.com

Peterhof
25, rue Bonaparte, 75006
peterhof.fr

Petit Bain
7, port de la Gare, 75013
petitbain.org

Pierre Hermé
Galeries Lafayette,
40, boulevard Haussmann, 75009
pierreherme.com

Piscine Joséphine-Baker
Quai François Mauriac, 75013
paris.fr

Point Éphémère
200, quai de Valmy, 75010
pointephemere.org

Pont des Arts
Quai du Louvre,
Place de l'Institut, 75006
paris.fr

Promenade Plantée
Quinze-Vingts, 75012
promenade-plantee.org

Rosa Bonheur
Parc des Buttes Chaumont,
2, avenue des Cascades, 75019
rosabonheur.fr

Rose Bakery
46, rue des Martyrs, 75009

Sacré Cœur
35, rue du Chevalier de la Barre,
75018
sacre-coeur-montmartre.com

St-Sulpice
26 bis, rue Cassette, 75006
paroisse-saint-sulpice-paris.org

**Salon de Thé de la Grande
Mosquée de Paris**
39, rue Geoffroy St-Hilaire,
75005
la-mosquee.com

Sébastien Gaudard
22, rue des Martyrs, 75009
sebastiengaudard.fr

Shakespeare & Company
37, rue de la Bûcherie, 75005
shakespeareandcompany.com

Stohrer
51, rue Montorgueil, 75002
stohrer.fr

Télescope
5, rue Villedo, 75001
telescopecafe.com

Verbano Traiteur
44, rue de Lancry, 75010

Water Bar
213, rue St-Honoré 75001
colette.fr

BIKE SHOPS, CLUBS, RACES AND VENUES

For links to our racing and
training routes, please visit
citycyclingguides.com

Bicycle Store
17, boulevard du Temple, 75003
bicyclestore.fr

Cycles Laurent
9, boulevard Voltaire, 75011
cycleslaurent.com

Cycles St-Honoré
156, rue St-Honore, 75001
cyclessainthonore.blogspot.
co.uk

En Selle Marcel
40, rue Tiquetonne, 75002
ensellemarcel.com

Freemoos
35, rue Pastourelle, 75003
freemoos.com

Gepetto & Vélos
59, rue du Cardinal Lemoine,
75005
gepetto-velos.com

Giant Store
1, boulevard Henri IV, 75004
giant-bicycles.com

Hippodrome de Longchamp
Route d'Auteuil aux Lacs, 75016
france-galop.com

L'Insep
11, avenue du Tremblay, 75012
insep.fr

Parc des Princes
24, rue du Commandant
Guilbaud, 75016
psg.fr

Paris Bike Co.
56, rue Gallieni,
92240 Malakoff
parisbikeco.com

Paris Cycles
Rond-Point du Jardin
d'Acclimatation, 75116
pariscycles.fr

Rando Cycles
5, rue Fernand Foureau, 75012
rando-cycles.com

Vélib
velib.paris.fr

**Vélodrome Municipal
Jacques Anquetil**
48, avenue de Gravelle,
94220 Charenton-le-Pont

OTHER USEFUL SITES

Eurostar
Gare du Nord,
18, rue de Dunkerque, 75010
eurostar.com

Métro
parismetro.com

RER
parisbytrain.com

TGV
tgv.com

Thalys
thalys.com

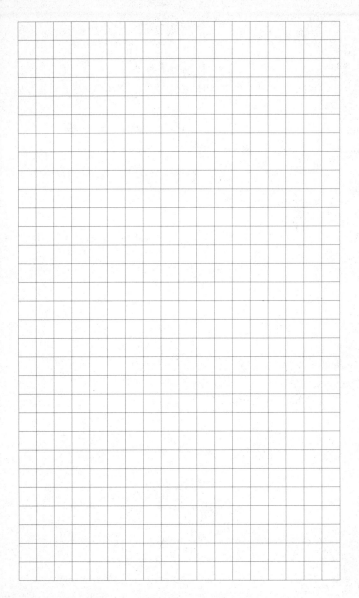

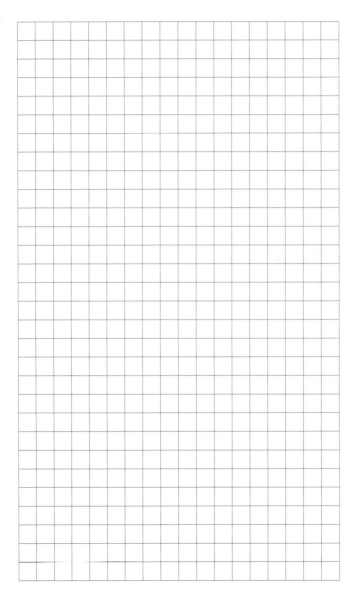

54

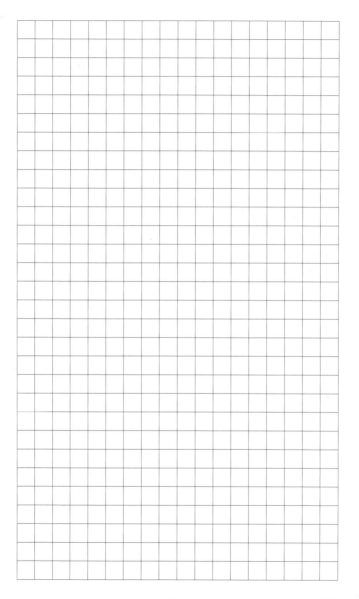

6 mins

½ km   ½ mile   1 km   1 mile

Ⓜ PONT DE LEVALLOIS BÉCON

Ⓜ ANATOLE FRANCE

Ⓜ LOUISE MICHEL

RÉFENSE

Ⓜ PONT DE NEUILLY

Ⓜ PON

Ⓜ LES SABLONS

Ⓜ PORTE MAILLOT
RER NEUILLY - PORTE MAILLOT
Ⓨ

Ⓜ ARGENTINE

Ⓜ PORTE DAUPHINE

Ⓜ

RER AV FOCH

Ⓜ VICTOR HUGO

Ⓜ BOISSIÈRE

16

RER AV HENRI MARTIN

Ⓜ RUE DE LA POMPE

Ⓜ TROCADÉRO

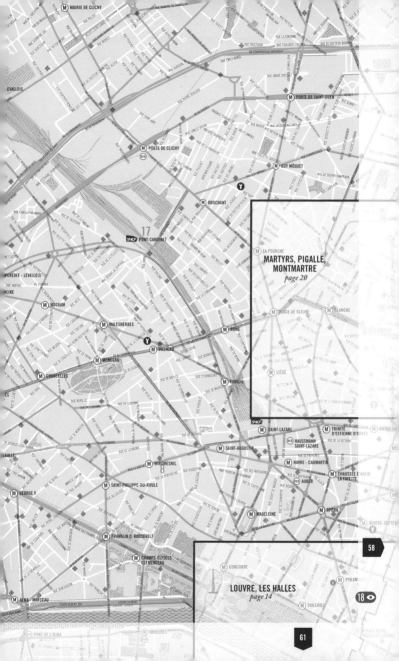

MARTYRS, PIGALLE, MONTMARTRE
page 20

LOUVRE, LES HALLES
page 14

58

18

61

M AUBERVILLIERS - PANTIN
QU~TRE CHEMINS

6 mins

½ km   ½ mile   1 km   1 mile

M PORTE DE LA VILLETTE

M PANTIN

M CORENTIN CARIOU

25

M ÉGLISE DE PANTIN

19

M HOCHE

M OURCQ

M DANUBE

M PRÉ-SAINT-GERVAIS

M MAIRIE DES LILAS

M BOTZARIS

M BUTTES CHAUMONT

M PL DES FÊTES

M PORTE DES LILAS

M JOURDAIN

M TÉLÉGRAPHE

M PYRÉNÉES

M SAINT-FARGEAU

M PELLEPORT

M MÉNILMONTANT

M GALLIENI

SAINT-MAUR

M GAMBETTA

M PORTE DE BAGNOLET

M PÈRE LACHAISE

M LA MUETTE
M PASSY
RER BOULAINVILLIERS
RER CHAMP DE MARS TOUR EIFFEL
M RANELAGH
RER BIR-HAKEIM
RER AV DU PRÉSIDENT KENNEDY
M JASMIN
M DUPL
M PORTE D'AUTEUIL
M MICHEL-ANGE AUTEUIL
M MIRABEAU
M ÉGLISE D'AUTEUIL
RER JAVEL
M JAVEL - ANDRÉ CITROËN
M CHARLES MICHEL
M MICHEL-ANGE MOLITOR
M CHARDON-LAGACHE
M EE
M FÉLIX FAURE
M EXELMANS
M BOUCICAUT
15
M PORTE DE SAINT-CLOUD
PONT DU GARIGLIANO
M LOURMEL
M BALARD
M PORTE DE VERSAILLES
RER ISSY - VAL DE SEINE
6 mins
¼ km   ½ mile   1 km   1 mile
M CORENTIN CELTON
M MAIRIE D'ISSY

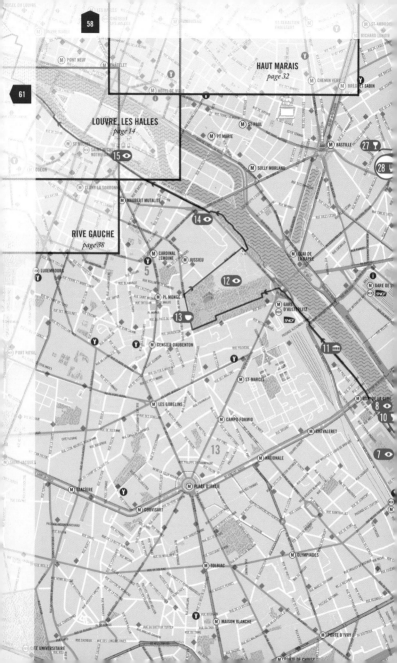

61

HAUT MARAIS
page 32

M PONT NEUF

CHÂTELET

M HÔTEL DE VILLE

M CHEMIN VERT

M BRÉGUET SABIN

LOUVRE, LES HALLES
page 14

M ST PAUL

M ST MICHEL

M SAINT MICHEL
NOTRE DAME

M PT MARIE

M BASTILLE

27

28

15

M SULLY MORLAND

M ODÉON

M CLUNY LA SORBONNE

M MAUBERT MUTALITÉ

14

RIVE GAUCHE
page 38

M CARDINAL
LEMOINE

M JUSSIEU

M QUAI DE
LA RAPÉE

5

LUXEMBOURG

12

M PL MONGE

M GARE
D'AUSTERLITZ
SNCF

i GARE DE L
M GARE DE L
SNCF

13

11

M CENSIER DAUBENTON

M PONT ROYAL

M ST-MARCEL

M LES GOBELINS

M CAMPO-FORMIO

M PONT DE LA GARE

8

10

M CHEVALERET

7

13

M NATIONALE

M GLACIÈRE

M PLACE D'ITALIE

M SAINT JACQUES

M CORVISART

M OLYMPIADES

M TOLBIAC

M MAISON BLANCHE

CITÉ UNIVERSITAIRE

M PORTE D'IVRY

M PORTE DE CHOISY

AIRE

Ⓜ PHILIPPE AUGUSTE

Ⓜ ALEXANDRE DUMAS

Ⓜ CHARONNE

Ⓜ RUE DES BOULETS

Ⓜ BUZENVAL

Ⓜ MARAICHERS

Ⓜ PTE DE MONTREUIL

Ⓜ AVRON

Ⓜ FAIDHERBE CHALIGNY

Ⓜ NATION

Ⓜ PORTE DE VINCENNES

Ⓜ REUILLY DIDEROT

Ⓜ SAINT-MANDÉ

Ⓜ PICPUS

Ⓜ MONTGALLET

12

③ 👁

Ⓜ BEL AIR

④ 👁

Ⓜ DAUMESNIL

Ⓜ DUGOMMIER

SNCF

Ⓜ MICHEL BIZOT

Ⓜ PORTE DORÉE

Ⓜ COUR ST EMILION

⑤ 👁

Ⓜ PORTE DE CHARENTON

Ⓜ LIBERTÉ

⑥ 👁

6 mins

¼ km   ½ mile   1 km   1 mile

Ⓜ CHARENTON - ÉCOLES

Rapha, established in London, has always been a champion of city cycling – from testing our first prototype jackets on the backs of bike couriers, to a whole range of products designed specifically for the demands of daily life on the bike. As well as an online emporium of products, films, photography and stories, Rapha has a growing network of Cycle Clubs, locations around the globe where cyclists can enjoy live racing, food, drink and products. Rapha is also the official clothing supplier of Team Sky, the world's leading cycling team.

Rapha.